WITHDRAWN

D1713615

MAGNETS

THIS EDITION
Editorial Management by Oriel Square
Produced for DK by WonderLab Group LLC
Jennifer Emmett, Erica Green, Kate Hale, *Founders*

Editors Grace Hill Smith, Libby Romero, Michaela Weglinski;
Photography Editors Kelley Miller, Annette Kiesow, Nicole di Mella; **Managing Editor** Rachel Houghton;
Designers Project Design Company; **Researcher** Michelle Harris; **Copy Editor** Lori Merritt;
Indexer Connie Binder; **Proofreader** Larry Shea; **Reading Specialist** Dr. Jennifer Albro;
Curriculum Specialist Elaine Larson

Published in the United States by DK Publishing
1745 Broadway, 20th Floor, New York, NY 10019

Copyright © 2023 Dorling Kindersley Limited
DK, a Division of Penguin Random House LLC
23 24 25 26 10 9 8 7 6 5 4 3 2 1
001-333874–June/2023

A catalog record for this book
is available from the Library of Congress.
HC ISBN: : 978-0-7440-7135-1
PB ISBN: 978-0-7440-7136-8

DK books are available at special discounts when purchased in bulk for sales promotions, premiums,
fundraising, or educational use. For details, contact: DK Publishing Special Markets,
1745 Broadway, 20th Floor, New York, NY 10019
SpecialSales@dk.com

Printed and bound in China

The publisher would like to thank the following for their kind permission to reproduce their images:
a=above; c=center; b=below; l=left; r=right; t=top; b/g=background

123RF.com: 1xpert 18crb, alphaspirit 28br; **Dorling Kindersley:** The Science Museum, London / Clive Streeter 25c, 25cr, 25cb, 25bl,
Whipple Museum of History of Science, Cambridge / Gary Ombler 24bc, 25cl; **Dreamstime.com:** 44Photography 18cb,
Beijing Hetuchuangyi Images Co., Ltd. 27tr, Chernetskaya 6t, Digikhmer 22br, Martin Fischer 25br, Fokinol 9cra, Haryigit 21t,
Jochenschneider 24bl, Roberto Junior 9crb, Dmitry Kalinovsky 28clb, Dimitar Marinov 15t, Andrey Navrotskiy 26ca,
Chatree Nuekngam 23t, Anton Petrychenko 10b, Photka 24cr, Pmakin 1cb, Robert Semnic 26tr, Verkoka 16t, Björn Wylezich 9cl;
Getty Images / iStock: gazanfer 3cb, 20cl; **NASA:** JPL 29br; **Shutterstock.com:** Emre Terim 23bl

Cover images: *Front and Spine:* **Dreamstime.com:** Sakkmesterke;
Back: **Dreamstime.com:** Ablvictoriya cra; **Shutterstock.com:** Lemono cla

All other images © Dorling Kindersley
For more information see: www.dkimages.com

For the curious
www.dk.com

MAGNETS

Roxanne Troup

Contents

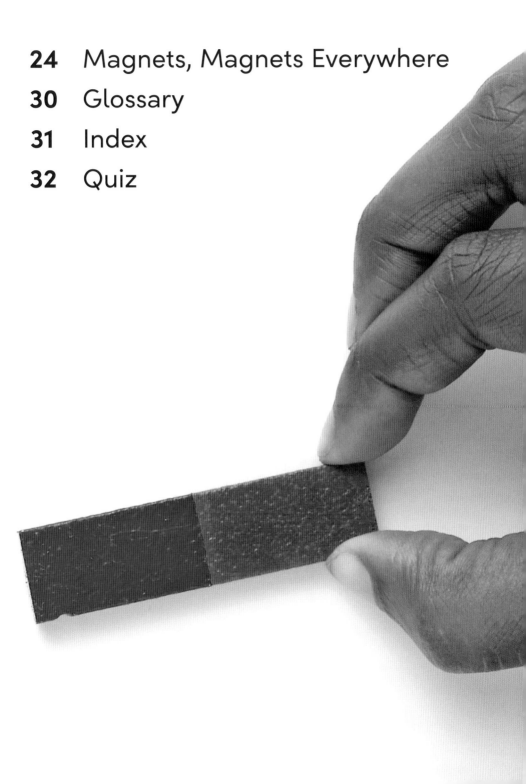

Is It Magic?

Magnets do amazing things. They attach paper to a refrigerator without tape. They move certain metals without touching them. Magnets can even make objects float. But these magnet tricks are not magic. They're science.

Try this. Take a magnet off your refrigerator. Test objects around your home to see what materials it responds to. Can your magnet pick up paper clips? How about toothpicks? Does it stick to your washing machine? A book? What about your bedroom doorknob?

The Science of Magic
Science helps magicians do magic tricks. All a magician needs for one cool trick is a pair of scissors and a large magnet. By placing the scissors on the table and the magnet under the table, the magician can move the scissors "with their mind" by sliding the magnet back and forth.

It's Science!

Magnets use an invisible force to move objects. This force is called magnetism. Magnetism attracts or pulls objects to a magnet. It can also repel or push objects away.

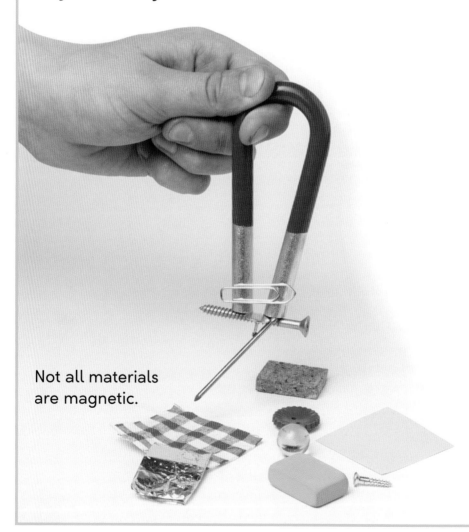

Not all materials are magnetic.

But magnets can only use this force on metals such as iron, cobalt, and nickel. Wood, glass, plastic, and copper are not attracted to magnets.

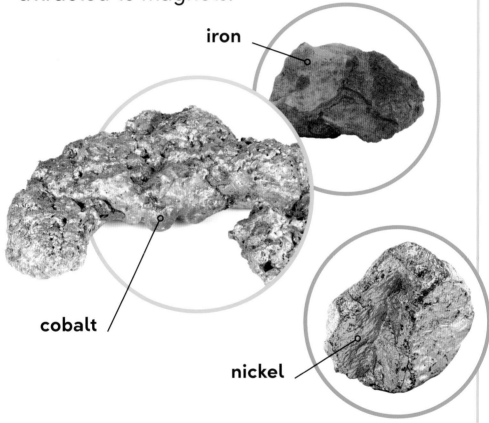

iron

cobalt

nickel

Magnetic Alloys
Some metal mixtures are also magnetic. But these alloys have to contain iron, cobalt, or nickel. Steel can be a magnetic alloy.

You can't see magnetism. But you can feel it. Lay two magnets side by side until they stick together. Pull the magnets apart. Then, see how close you can hold them without letting them touch. Do you feel that pull?

Now turn one magnet around. Try your experiment again. Hold the magnets close together. Don't let them touch! Do you feel that push?

The area around a magnet that pushes and pulls objects near it is called a magnetic field. Stronger magnets create bigger magnetic fields.

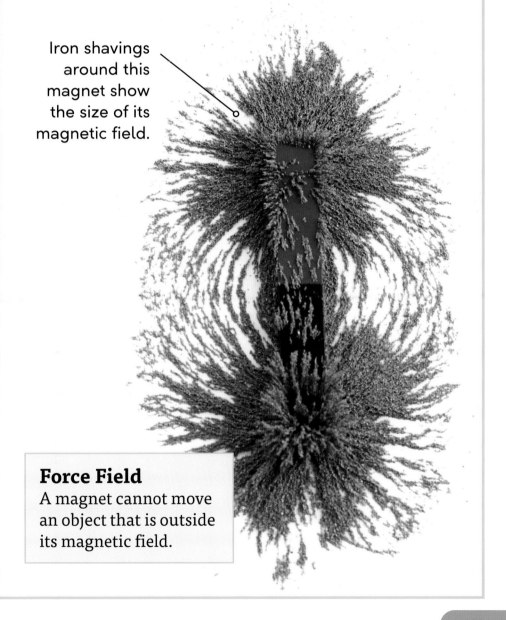

Iron shavings around this magnet show the size of its magnetic field.

Force Field
A magnet cannot move an object that is outside its magnetic field.

How Magnets Work

The strongest parts of any magnet are its poles. All magnets have two ends or poles—a north pole and a south pole. Even if you cut a magnet in half, it will still have two poles. Its magnetic field will just be smaller.

One Giant Magnet
Molten iron spins inside Earth's core, creating a magnetic field. Earth has a north pole and a south pole, too. Our planet is one giant magnet!

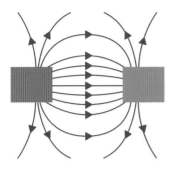

opposite poles attract

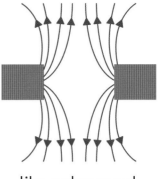

like poles repel

In magnets, opposite poles attract and like poles repel. Place the north pole of one magnet near the south pole of another, and the magnets will pull together. But place the south pole of one magnet near the south pole of another, and the magnets will push apart.

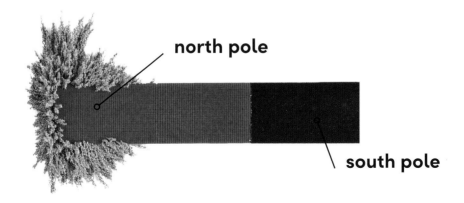

north pole

south pole

All matter is made up of tiny pieces called atoms. Inside atoms are even smaller pieces, some of which carry electric charges. These pieces are called electrons. Electrons spin around the center of an atom, creating a current. This current makes each electron magnetic. But that does not make the atom magnetic—yet.

Most atoms have equal numbers of electrons that spin in opposite directions. This cancels out the atom's magnetic force. But in some atoms, electrons spin in the same direction. This makes the atom magnetic. When several magnetic atoms are grouped together, they create a magnetic domain. An object with magnetic domains can be made into a magnet.

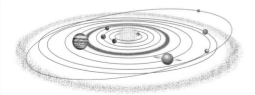

Like planets orbiting the Sun, electrons spin and orbit the nucleus, or center, of an atom.

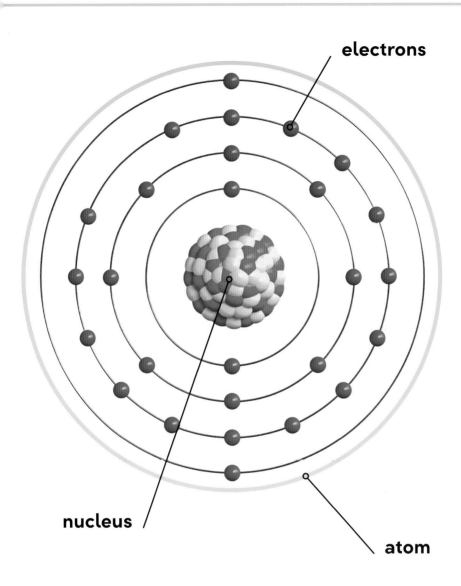

electrons

nucleus

atom

Magnets in the Making

Nearly all the electrons in iron, cobalt, and nickel spin in the same direction. That's why these materials make good magnets.

Tug-of-war is a battle of force.
The side with the greatest force wins.

Usually the magnetic domains in an object pull in different directions. This cancels out an object's magnetism. Imagine playing tug-of-war with your friends. It's hard to win when both sides use equal force to pull the rope in different directions. But what happens when one side gets a few extra players? It wins!

The same thing happens when magnetic domains line up. The force of the domains' magnetism grows stronger. If enough domains line up and start pulling in the same direction, the material will become a magnet.

Lining It Up

Manufacturers use electromagnets to force the magnetic domains in iron, cobalt, and nickel to line up and make a permanent magnet. (*Learn about electromagnets on page 21.*)

1. The magnetic domains are not lined up.

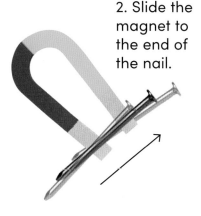

Try this out. Find a nail, some paper clips, and a magnet. Place one pole of your magnet against the side of your nail. Slide the magnet to the end of the nail. Repeat this 30 times—always in the same direction. Touch your nail to a paper clip. Does it attract? You just made a magnet!

2. Slide the magnet to the end of the nail.

3. The magnetic domains are now lined up.

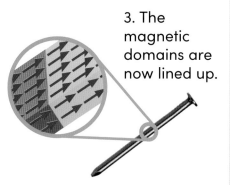

Types of Magnets

There are two types of magnets: permanent magnets and temporary magnets. Permanent magnets hold a magnetic charge for a long time. Temporary magnets do not. The magnets on your refrigerator are permanent magnets.

Strength Test
The strength of a magnetic field is measured in a unit called a gauss. Mathematician Carl Friedrich Gauss was the first to measure the strength of Earth's magnetism.

Permanent magnets do not last forever, though. They can be damaged by high heat or when dropped. Their magnetic charge can also "leak" over time. Magnetism flows in a loop from the north to south poles. But it flows best through magnetic material. When magnetism flows through air to return to a magnet's north pole, it loses a bit of strength.

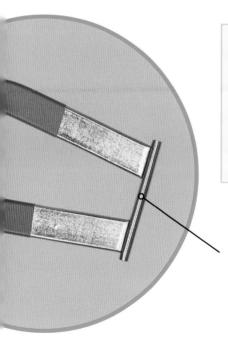

Magnet Storage
Store magnets in a wood or plastic container. Keep them cool, and stack them with opposite poles touching. This will help them last.

The bar on this horseshoe magnet is called a keeper. It connects the magnet's poles and keeps the magnetic charge from "leaking" out.

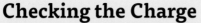

Checking the Charge
Test your nail-magnet again.
(See page 17.) Can it still pick
up a paper clip? Probably not.
But you can recharge it.
It's a temporary magnet.

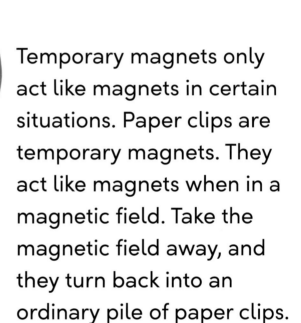

Temporary magnets only act like magnets in certain situations. Paper clips are temporary magnets. They act like magnets when in a magnetic field. Take the magnetic field away, and they turn back into an ordinary pile of paper clips.

Paper clips act like little magnets when attached to a permanent magnet.

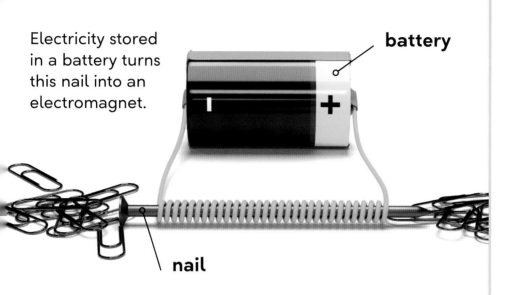

Electricity stored in a battery turns this nail into an electromagnet.

battery

nail

Electromagnets are a special type of temporary magnet. They are made with electricity. Electricity flowing through a wire creates a weak magnetic field. Wrap that wire around a piece of iron, and the iron becomes a magnet. Wrap it tighter, and the magnet gets stronger. But turn the electricity off, and the iron rod loses its magnetism.

The Discovery

William Sturgeon created the first electromagnet in 1825 using a horseshoe-shaped piece of iron and a piece of wire. His small electromagnet could lift nine pounds (4 kg).

Powering Our Lives

Electromagnets are very useful. They power all electric motors and come in different shapes and sizes. You can find small electromagnets in earbuds and electric toothbrushes. Large electromagnets help sort and move metal piles in recycling centers. Electromagnets make doorbells work. They run appliances and even store data in computers.

Electromagnets also create electricity. You know that as electrons spin around an atom, they create a magnetic charge. But when electrons jump between atoms, they create an electric charge. Magnetism pushes these jumping electrons in the same direction, producing electricity.

A Quick Charge
Electricity travels close to the speed of light! Electricity is measured in volts.

Electromagnets help power a hydroelectric dam, which provides electricity to a town.

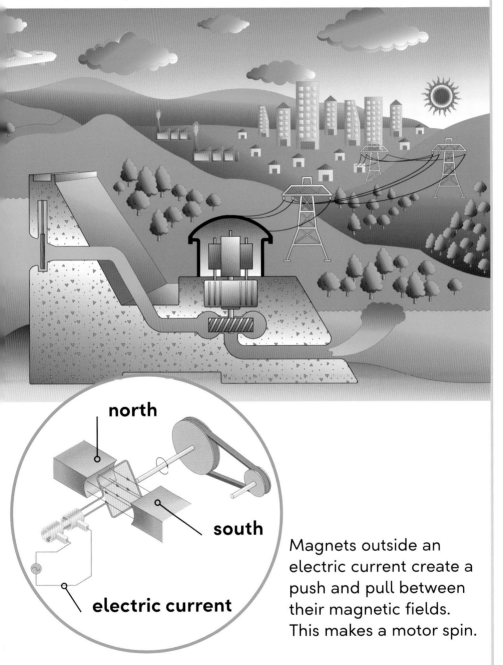

north

south

electric current

Magnets outside an electric current create a push and pull between their magnetic fields. This makes a motor spin.

Magnets, Magnets Everywhere

Long ago, humans discovered a "magic" rock. Iron stuck to it. And when it hung from a string, it pointed north. Ancient explorers used this rock to make the first compass. They called it a lodestone or "guide stone."

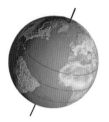

William Gilbert uses lodestone to experiment with electricity and magnets and theorizes that Earth is a magnet

Humans discover lodestone

 600   221–206   1200   1600   1752

◀ BCE | CE ▶

Chinese explorers invent the first compass

Use of the compass spreads to Europe

Benjamin Franklin's kite experiment shows the connection between lightning and electricity

Today, we know that Earth has a magnetic field. It protects us from the Sun's harmful rays. We also know that many animals use magnetism to migrate far. It allows them to travel without getting lost.

Alessandro Volta creates the first battery

William Sturgeon creates the first electromagnet

Electromagnetic research leads to inventions of the telegraph, radio, electric motor, telephone, and power plant

| 1799 | 1820 | 1825 | 1831 | 1834–1895 | Today |

Hans Christian Oersted discovers the connection between electricity and magnetism

Michael Faraday builds the first generator

Researchers experiment to create stronger, smaller, and lighter magnets

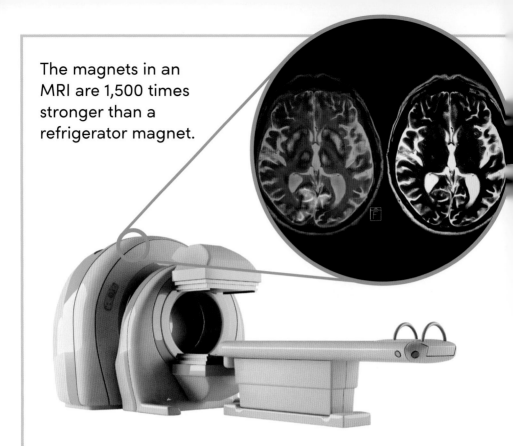

The magnets in an MRI are 1,500 times stronger than a refrigerator magnet.

Today, we use magnets in many different ways. Magnets are used in medicine.

A magnetic resonance imaging (MRI) machine allows doctors to "see" inside a human body without hurting their patient. MRIs use magnets to briefly move atoms in the body. A computer measures that movement and creates an image of the inside of the body. Doctors use MRI images to diagnose their patients.

With less friction, maglev trains can travel up to 375 miles per hour (600 kph).

Magnets improve travel. A maglev train "floats" above a set of tracks. One set of magnets pushes the train up. Another set pushes it forward. Since the train does not rub against the tracks, it goes really fast!

Other Vehicles

Electromagnets power electric cars. They also help power airplanes and submarines.

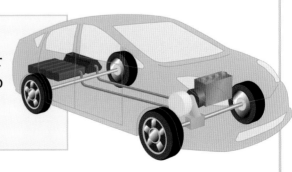

Magnets are important to technology and communication, too. Magnets allow computers to store a lot of information in a small space. They power speakers and help collect renewable energy.

Without magnets, wind energy could not be converted into electricity.

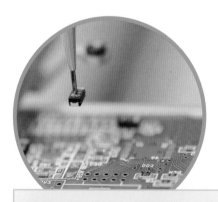

Magnets to Microchips
Esther Marley Conwell's work in magnet science led to the creation of the microchip. Microchips allow computer engineers to build smaller computers.

New uses for magnets are being developed all the time—even in space. NASA uses magnets to explore other planets. Researchers think magnets could also help clean up space junk. Or even let spaceships land on an asteroid. With all we've already learned about magnets, who knows what else we'll discover?

NASA uses magnets on Mars Pathfinder to learn more about Mars.

Glossary

Atoms
The building blocks of all matter

Attract
To pull something closer

Electromagnet
Magnet made with electricity

Electrons
Tiny particles that move inside an atom and carry an electric charge

Magnetic domain
A group of magnetic atoms

Magnetic field
The area around a magnet that pushes and pulls objects within its field

Magnetism
An invisible force that pushes or pulls certain metals when near a magnet

Migrate
Moving from one area to another, especially tied to a specific time of year

Permanent magnet
A long-lasting magnet

Pole
The end of a magnet

Repel
To push something away

Temporary magnet
A magnet that cannot hold a magnetic charge for long periods of time

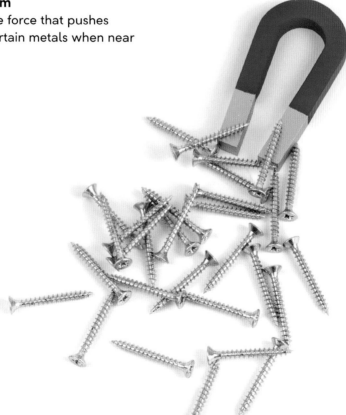

Index

Quiz

Answer the questions to see what you have learned. Check your answers in the key below.

1. What materials can magnets attract?

2. Where are the strongest points on a magnet?

3. True or False: The Earth is a magnet.

4. How many kinds of magnets are there?

5. What is the difference between permanent and temporary magnets?

6. What is an electromagnet?

7. Name three things electromagnets are used for.

8. What is lodestone?

1. Iron, cobalt, and nickel 2. At its poles 3. True 4. Two: permanent and temporary 5. Permanent magnets hold their charge for a long time, and temporary magnets do not 6. A magnet made with electricity 7. Answers could include electric motors, earbuds, speakers, electric toothbrushes, doorbells, appliances, data storage, creating electricity, MRIs, and maglev trains 8. A naturally occurring magnet